EPIC SONG

EPIC SONG

PABLO NERUDA

Translated by
Richard Schaaf

Azul Editions

Originally published in Spanish by Editorial El Siglo Ilustrado,
Montevideo, Uruguay, under the title *Canción de gesta*, copyright
Editorial El Siglo Ilustrado.

Originally translated into English by Miguel Algarín under the
title *Song of Protest*, published by William Morrow & Company,
Inc., New York, 1976.

This edition published by
Azul Editions
7804 Sycamore Drive
Falls Church, VA 22042
USA
azulpress@aol.com

ISBN 1-885214-15-4

Library of Congress Catalog Number: 98-72736

Printed in the United States of America

First Edition
10 9 8 7 6 5 4 3 2 1

CONTENTS

Meditation on the Sierra Maestra

PROLOGUE

At first this book was centered around Puerto Rico, her agonizing colonial condition, the struggle of her insurgent patriots. Later, with the magnanimous events in Cuba, the scope of the book broadened and developed throughout the Caribbean.

Therefore, I dedicate it to the liberators of Cuba: to Fidel Castro, his comrades and the Cuban people. I also dedicate it to those in Puerto Rico and throughout the sizzling Caribbean world who fight for freedom and truth always threatened by the United States of North America.

This book is not a solitary lament or an emanation from darkness; rather, it is a weapon aimed point-blank, a basic and fraternal aid that I offer my sister Caribbean nations in their daily struggles.

Those who went to great lengths to reproach me before will continue to reproach me even more. For my part, I here assume with pride my duties as poet of public utility—that is, a pure poet. Poetry has always flowed with the purity of water and fire which cleans or burns, unavoidably and unrelentingly.

I sincerely hope that my poetry serves my Caribbean sisters and brothers in their honorable duties. All over America there remains much for us to clean and burn.

Much must be constructed.

May each and every one of us through sacrifice win what is ours. Only then will we be truly happy.

Our peoples have suffered so much that we will have given them very little when we have given them all.

—*Pablo Neruda*
Aboard the freighter *Louis Lumière* between America and Europe, 12 April 1960.

PROLOGUE IN 1968 TO THE
THIRD URUGUAYAN EDITION

It is now known that I wrote this book in 1960. Since then I have traveled throughout the Americas reading it to large and small audiences. In my country, Chile, I have read its songs of the Cuban epic from the northern desert to beyond the Strait of Magellan. Mexico and Peru heard these verses. Students and workers were the majority of my spirited public. When invited by P.E.N. in the United States to one of its congresses, I read my lyric, epic and anti-imperialist poetry before many large audiences in New York and California.

Some literary Cubans drafted and disseminated a letter against me that will pass into infamy. Printed in Madrid, in printshops authorized by Franco, with the postal image of the fascist dictator, it was distributed by the thousands in Latin America. It was also given a costly and enormous distribution in Europe and Asia.

Epic Song is still ardently alive in its many editions. It was the first book that any poet—in Cuba or anywhere else—had dedicated to the Cuban Revolution.

In authorizing this new Uruguayan edition, I believe that those who will read these poems in years to come will judge our epoch and arrive at their own thoughts about the work and lives of one another.

Meanwhile my passion and my work will continue, as in this book, strengthening and defending the Cuban Revolution in spite of its literary Cains. It is the great historical event that has importance in our peoples' journey, and history will not concern itself with bitter resentments nor the resentful.

Therefore, I swear my poetry will continue serving and singing of dignity against the indignant, of hope to the despairing, of justice in spite of injustice, of equality in spite of the exploiters, of truth against the liars and of the great fraternity of true combatants.

—Pablo Neruda
Isla Negra, 1968

Neruda had learned that the Cuban writers Roberto Fernández Retamar, Edmundo Desnoes and Lisandro Otero were behind this slanderous letter. Whether true or not, Neruda understood that revolutions do at times cause revolutionaries and counterrevolutionaries alike to make mistakes and fall into error. However in his memoirs, written much later and long after this ideological feud between Communist Parties was resolved, Neruda somewhat self-critical of his own pride confesses that he continued to refuse to shake hands with those who knowingly or unknowingly signed the letter. (Translator's Note)

EPIC SONG

I

PUERTO RICO, PUERTO POBRE

I know it is late now to begin,
but I feel this is what I must do:
now as before I come forth
to sing or to die: now I will begin.
There's no force that can silence me
but for the sad magnitude of time
and its ally: death with its plow
for the sowing of bones.
I've chosen a subject boiling over
with blood, with palm trees and silence,
about an island surrounded by
many waters and endless death:
a river of lamentation bleeds there
and the sorrow of those who wait mounts.
It is a poor, imprisoned island
where ashen days come and go,
where the light soars and descends on the palms,
where night travels in its black ship
and there she is, there's the prisoner,
the island engulfed in suffering.
And our blood bleeds into hers
because a golden claw tears from her
her lovers and her birthright.

II

MUÑOZ MARÍN

There exists a gluttonous worm in these waters,
a predatory worm:
he devoured the island's flag
and hoisted in its place his overseer's banner,
nourishing himself with the prisoner blood
of her poor buried patriots.
The worm fattened up
on the golden crown of American wheat,
prospering in the shade of money,
bloodied with tortures and soldiers,
inaugurating false monuments,
turning land passed down from
father to father into enslaved property,
turning an island as clear and bright as a star
into a cramped grave for slaves,
and this tapeworm lived among the poets,
defeated in their own exile,
ordering respect for his teachers,
paying pythagorean Peruvians
to propagate his government,
and his palace was pure white on the outside
and inside it was a hell like Chicago,
where lived the mustache, the heart, the claws
of that traitor Luis Muñoz, the Worm,

Muñoz Marín to his audience,
Judas of the bleeding territory,
governor of the island's yoke,
corrupter of his poor brothers,
bilingual translator for executioners,
chauffeur of North American whiskey.

III

HERE'S WHAT'S HAPPENING

The arching arrow of these years is smiling
and our offended America is miserable.
Man reaches into space in his capsule
staking his claim on the moon
while Nicaragua rots
in a worm infested dynasty
dishonoring the blood of Sandino,
the seed of Rubén Darío.
Oh Nicaragua, heart of the swan,
bloodline of a raging rapier,
lift your breast and your voice,
raise the angry sword of your life
and in blood and fire cut loose the manacles
that crown your lineage with thorns.
This is how the emerald,
the waistline, the Indian coast
of slender America is seen,
extending to the radiant green of the islands,
where a poor and bloody island lies:
half a radiant island.
For thirty years Trujillo's
teeth gnawed at her wound,
thirty years without peace or moon,
without shadow, without sun, only misery
for when man destroyed all wonder with gunfire

and perhaps, finally, all existence of kings,
exquisite and star-studded,
like a spiderweb of pain
anger persists in the Americas
alongside the wrath of the poor and naked,
alongside the greed and excesses of the tyrant,
while Muñoz of Puerto Pobre
forges his island's signature
and under the pirate's skull-and-crossbones
sells out language, reason, land and happiness,
sells out the honor of our poor America,
sells out parents and grandparents and ashes.

IV

CUBA APPEARS

When torture and darkness
seem to deaden the free air
and you see not the wave's spume
but blood among the reefs,
Fidel's hand reaches forth and in it
Cuba, pure rose of the Caribbean.
Thus history with her light teaches us
man can change that which exists,
and if he carries purity into battle
a noble spring will blossom to honor him:
left behind is the night of the tyrant,
his cruelty, his insensible eyes,
all the gold seized by his claws,
his mercenaries, his cannibal judges,
his lofty monuments sustained
by torment, dishonor and crime:
everything falls to dust
when the people raise their violins,
face forward and interrupt and sing—
interrupt the hatred of shadows and watchdogs,
sing the stars awake with their song—
riddling the darkness with gunfire.
Thus Fidel reached out through the shadows
so the jasmine tree may be born.

V

THE EPIC

If the ocean's depths silenced her pain,
the earth lifted her hopes
that disembarked on the coast:
they were the arms and fists of the struggle:
Fidel Castro with fifteen of his comrades
and freedom advancing on the sand.
The island was dark as though in mourning,
but they raised a banner of light
with dawn as their only weapon
and dawn still slept behind the earth.
Then in silence they started the struggle
clearing a pathway toward the stars.
Exhausted yet determined they pressed on
for honor and duty to war
with blood as their only weapon—
they were naked as newborns.
Thus Cuba's freedom was born
from that handful of men on the sand.
Then the dignity of naked men
dressed them in the clothes of the sierra,
fed them anonymous bread,
armed them with clandestine gunpowder,
and those asleep woke up with them,
seething offenses sprang up from the grave,

mothers sent their children off,
the peasant spoke up of his misery,
and the pure army of the poor
grew and grew like the full moon—
no soldiers were lost in battle,
the canefields thrived in the storm,
the enemy abandoned their weapons
on the cart paths and roads,
the executioners trembled and fell,
undone by the spring, by gunfire
that finally pinned death to their shirts,
while like the wind, like the windswept prairies,
the movement of a free people
moved, shook the island's furrows, surged
and swelled over the sea like a planet.

VI

ANCIENT HISTORY

Now I open my eyes and remember:
the bitter and magical history of Cuba
sparkles and dims, electric and dark,
with euphoria and with suffering.
Years passed the way fish pass
through the bountiful blue and sweetness of the sea—
the island lived in freedom and in dance,
the palm trees were dancing in the salt spray,
blacks and whites were a single loaf of bread
because Martí kneaded their fermenting dough,
peace fulfilled its golden destiny,
the sun crackled in the sugar,
while a ray of sun-ripened honey
fell over the fruit:
mankind was content with his reign
and the family with its agriculture,
when from the north a threatening,
covetous and unjust seed arrived
to spin its web like a spider
and construct a metallic structure,
to sink bloody nails into the land
and erect a vault over the dead.
It was the yellow-toothed dollar,
commander of blood and grave.

VII

CENTRAL LAND

The Americas join
where two oceans marry—
from the Atlantic they gather the wave's spume,
from the Pacific torrential stars—
ships from the white poles arrived
filled with oil and orange blossoms.
These seafaring warehouses swallowed up
our secret mineral blood,
which erects skyscrapers over the planet
in cruel and spiny cities.
Thus the empire of the dollar
and its sinister family was established:
bloody Caribbean cannibals
disguised as heroic generals,
merciless mice,
an inheritance of armed spit,
a stinking cavern of imperious orders,
a gutter of tropical sewage,
a dark chain of torment,
a rosary of insufferable misery
while the dollar is at the helm of
immorality's white fleet on the seas
expropriating the aroma of the plaintain,
the richness of coffee,

sustaining bloodstained Trujillos
in our pure lands.
Poor America up to her waist
in blood in so many slums,
crucified on the cross, with thorns,
handcuffed, gnawed at by dogs,
ripped to shreds by invaders,
wounded by torture and outrage,
lashed by false winds,
sacriligious deals, massive plundering.
Oh narrow chain of sorrows,
Oh meeting place for the rush of tears of two oceans.

VIII

ALSO IN THE SOUTH

The universal carnation of our republics
have been bled dry in prisons:
Cuba's heart was emptied
by Batista's executioners
and before, Ubico had imposed on Guatemala
the tragic iron lock of greed.
Across the broadest expanses on the planet—
mountains, yellow Patagonian wastelands,
snow-capped volcanoes,
equatorial rivers throbbing
in the Amazonian regions—
tyranny leaves its scars
on Paraguay's shattered walls
and Bolivia's bitter stones.

IX

I REMEMBER A MAN

Speaking of the torrid palms
the Caribbean kisses and lashes,
I will say that among the many black eyes
those of Martí were the most courageous.
He could see near and far
and even now his vision is radiant
as if time could not diminish its energy.
The eyes of Cuba are born.
Back then it was grueling, dirty work
to raise an independent laurel,
to dream of freedom
was life-threatening.
But Martí armed with hope and with guns
awakened the daydreamer and the peasant
and constructed with blood and thought
the architecture of the dawning light.

X

THAT FRIEND

After Sandino crossed the jungle
he unloaded his blessed gunpowder
against the invading sailors
trained and paid for in New York.
The earth caught fire, the foliage resounded,
the Yankee hadn't expected this.
He came well-dressed for war,
shoes and weapons shining like new.
But experience soon taught him
who Sandino and Nicaragua were
for everything spelled a tomb for the blond thieves—
the air, the trees, the roads, the water.
Sandino's guerrillas were even
in the whiskey which brought on
sickness and sudden death
for those glorious fighters from Louisiana
accustomed to lynching blacks
with superhuman courage—
two thousand hooded men working
over one black man, a rope and a tree.
Yes, business was different here:
Sandino attacked, retreated, then waited.
Sandino was the coming night,
he was the light from the sea that killed.

Sandino was a tower of patriotic flags.
Sandino was a rifle of hope—
Yes, these were very different lessons.
At West Point things were neat and clean,
the cadets were never taught
that he who kills could die.
North Americans never understood
our love for our poor beloved land,
and how we will defend our flags
sown of pain and love.
If they didn't learn this in Philadelphia
they learned it with their blood in Nicaragua.
The captain of the people waited there,
Augusto C. Sandino was his name.
And in this song his name will remain
wondrous as a sudden fiery blaze
to shine its light on us, to shine its fire on us
in the continuation of his battles.

XI

TREASON

On a tragic night for peace
General Sandino was invited
to dine, to celebrate his courage,
with the "American" Ambassador
(since these pirates have usurped
the name of the whole continent).
General Sandino was in good spirits,
wine and drinks were raised to his health.
The Yankees were headed back home
decisively defeated
and this banquet sealed the struggle
of Sandino and his brothers with honor.
The assassin sat waiting at his table,
a sly spineless being,
toasting to Sandino again and again
while the hidious thirty dollars
for the crime resounded in his pockets.
Oh banquet of bloody wine!
Oh night, oh false moonlit pathways!
Oh yellow stars that did not speak up!
Oh mute land, blinded by the night!
Earth that did not halt his horse!
Oh treacherous night that betrayed
his tower of honor into evil hands!

Oh banquet of silver and agony!
Oh premeditated, treasonous shadow!
Oh pavilion of light that once flourished,
and that since then is defeated and mourned!

XII

DEATH

Sandino rose to leave unaware
his victory had come to an end,
that when the ambassador pointed him out
he was fulfilling his part of the contract.
Everything was arranged for the crime
between the assassin and the North American.
There in the doorway as they embraced him
and saw him off, they were condemning him.
Congratulations! And Sandino left
walking with the executioner and death.

XIII

THE TRAITOR DIES

The traitor's name was Somoza:
mercenary, tyrant, executioner.
I say "was" because one day
a ray of light nailed him against the wall.
Nicaragua knows martyrdoms,
its soul held in shackles,
while her leaders wrote
with greedy pens, in a mule's voice,
comparing Somoza to God, to the planets,
to the rosy hue of dawn,
while he strangled Nicaragua
with his thief's hands and sly fingers.
Then, brave Rigoberto Lopez turned up:
he found Somoza rejoicing at his affairs
and with a burst of raging gunfire
cut short the traitor's life.
Thus fell the perforated Abdomen
and honor was restored.
The hero who delivered the blow died right there,
he had sowed his destiny with his fists.
His deed was his seed of death!
May the canticle of the world honor his name!

XIV

DYNASTIES

But from the spilled guts
came little Somozas,
two clowns splattered in blood,
from the cruel frog two fertile tadpoles.
Scarcely had the purulent one rotted
than two idiot generals ascended:
they embroidered themselves with diamonds
declared themselves lifetime presidents
parceled all the haciendas between themselves
fashioned themselves as *nouveaux riches*
and made themselves the favorite warriors
of the North American ambassador.
This is how history is made in our land,
how crimes are perpetuated,
and the chain of the terrible remains unbroken
and the military's dark reign of terror continues.

XV

I COME FROM THE SOUTH

I was born to sing these sorrows,
to expose the vermin,
to examine impudence with a ray of light,
to touch inhuman scars.
I am of American parentage,
born of Araucanian ashes,
for when the invader came seeking gold
my country advanced fire and pain against him.
In other lands he dressed in gold,
but here the conqueror did not conquer:
insatiable Pedro de Valdivia
found what he was looking for in my country—
he died under a cinnamon tree
his mouth stuffed with melted gold.
I represent the tribes that fell
defending their beloved banners
and nothing remained but silence and rain
after the splendor of their battles,
but I continue their actions
and throughout America
I stir up my people's sorrow,
I incite the root of their blades,
I embrace the memory of their heroes,
I water their subterranean hopes:
I mean, what purpose does my song serve—
this gift of beauty and words—

if it doesn't serve my people
to fight and walk with me?
Thus I go throughout our dark Americas
igniting fuses and lamps.
Tyrants deny me visas
because they are threatened by my poetry,
and if they bolt shut their doors against me
I enter like the light, through windows,
and if they inflame their territories against me,
I enter down their flowing rivers.
My poetry finds it way even into prisons
to speak with the one who waits for me,
and with the fugitive I count the stars
all night, and in the morning I leave.
The ocean reefs do not block me,
machine guns do not stop me,
my poetry has the eyes of dawn,
fists of stone and a winged heart.
When people recognize me on the street,
in copper mines or in barley fields,
from trains crossing the countryside,
on bittersweet plantations,
if people greet me in distant ports
or in infernal subterranean mines,
it is because my poetry has passed that way
with its wheel of love and vengeance
to establish clarity in the world
to give light to those who hope for it
to bring victory to those who struggle for it
to give the earth to those who work it.

XVI

IN GUATEMALA

As in Sandino's time
I saw the rose open in Guatemala.
I saw the poor man's soil defended
and justice arrive every month.
Arbenz opened his gentle and
powerful hand among his people
and the schools became granaries
of triumphant possiblities . . .
until from the Canal far-reaching claws
ripped clear across dawn's pathway.
The North American firemongers
dropped dollars and bombs:
death established its finery,
United Fruit uncoiled its rope.
Thus Guatemala was murdered
in full flight, like a dove.

XVII

IN EL SALVADOR, DEATH

In El Salvador death still patrols.
The blood of dead peasants
hasn't dried, time hasn't dried it,
the rain hasn't washed it from the roads.
Fifteen thousand were mowed down.
Martínez was the murderer's name.
And since then the soil, the bread and wine
in El Salvador tastes of blood.

XVIII

FREEDOM

Treasures of the Caribbean, renowned spume
spilt over illustrious blues,
fragrant coastlines that appear made of
silver and gold, embroidered sand,
archipelago of intense dreams,
region of murmurs and outbursts,
castles of floating palm trees,
mountains like perfumed pineapples,
melodious islands that arrive to the dance
of the wind like invited brides,
races the color of night and wood,
eyes like star-filled nights,
statues that dance in the forests
as the waves make love to the sea,
saffron hips that carry
the rhythm of love through the branches,
breasts dark as rustic smoke
smelling of jasmine in thatched huts,
wild hair twisting through the shade,
smiles the moon would edify,
coconut trees yielding to the wind,
people as agreeable and mellow as guitars,
poverty of islands and coasts,
men without land, children without spoons,
lithe girls girating

to a deep African drum,
dark heroes of the coffee fields,
hard workers in the canefields,
children of water, fathers of sugar,
athletes of oil and bananas,
oh bountiful Caribbean of dazzling gifts,
oh land and sea splattered with blood,
oh Antilles destined for Heaven,
abused by the devil and by man,
now the hour of hours has come,
the hour of dawn:
and he who tries to annihilate the light
will fall severed from life.
When I say the hour has come
I mean freedom reconquered,
I mean a seed grows in Cuba
a thousand times a thousand loved and awaited,
I mean the seed of our dignity
for so long wounded and trampled under
falls into the furrow, and the flags of
America's revolution rise into the day.

XIX

TO FIDEL CASTRO

Fidel, Fidel, the people thank you
for your words in action and deeds that sing,
which is why I brought you from far off
a cup of my country's wine:
it is the blood of a subterranean people
reaching from the darkness to your throat,
miners who have lived for centuries
extracting fire from the frozen earth.
They go down under the ocean for coal
and when they emerge they're like ghosts—
they have adapted to eternal night,
the workday light was robbed from them.
Nevertheless here is this cup full of
so much suffering and so much distance:
the happiness of men imprisoned
clinging to darkness and hope
who from deep in the mines know
when spring and its fragrances arrive
because they know man is struggling
to attain the most ample clarity.
And Cuba is seen by the miners in the far south,
solitary sons of the pampa,
shepherds of the cold in Patagonia,
fathers of tin and silver,
those who marry the cordillera,

extract copper from Chuquicamata,
anonymous men hunkered in buses
among populations of pure nostalgia,
women in the fields, in the workshops,
children who cried all through their childhood—
here, this is the cup, take it, Fidel.
It is full of so much hope
that upon drinking from it you will know
your victory is like my country's aged wine
grown not by one man but by many men,
not from one grape but from many vines,
not one drop but many rivers,
not one captain but many battles.
They all support you because you embody
our dignity in the long struggle,
and if Cuba were to fall we would all fall,
and we would all come to lift her up,
and if Cuba flourishes with all her flowers,
she will flourish with our own nectar.
And if they dare lay a finger on Cuba's
forehead, liberated by your own hands,
they will encounter the fists of the people,
we will raise our buried weapons,
and our blood and our pride will come
to the defense of our beloved Cuba.

XX

RETURNING TO PUERTO POBRE

While laurels are placed on Cuba's
victories, brilliant the world over,
an arrow pierces my soul
and my concern returns to Puerto Rico.
Now that our peoples have sung
why suddenly was the mortal chain
of her silence like a wound?
When freedom was won in Cuba
flags waved in the wind,
but one sister flag was missing—
the colors of your people were missing.
When each nation sang its song
of victory and suffering,
and each national voice recited its verse,
you lowered your eyes in silence.
Even Muñoz, the Liar, sent his acceptance
telegram infused with fear,
but your voice was in prison,
your poor heart a prisoner.
The North American put his foot down
and issued Muñoz a decree:
under that decree and under that foot
the Free Associated State reeks of death.
Associated Muñoz paces up and down
the corridors of the Department

offering poor Puerto Rico
a coffin full of bloodstained dollars.
Ay! poor Puerto Rico Puerto Pobre!
nailed by your traitorous sons
with nails of torture that shatter
your bones on a cross of dollars.
Still, I announce your new day,
I announce the arrival of your time:
the mercenaries will writhe in the dust,
your suffering will be crowned,
your dignity, your own voice and
own thoughts will be restored:
you will remove forever Chicago's banners
and your flag will wave free in the wind.

XXI

AMBUSHES

Nowadays it seems poisonous lies
mount against Cuba,
the wires are filled with them day and night
preparing for the moment of attack:
"It seems the Church is distrustful,"
"There is discontent in Cayo Benito,"
"Fidel didn't show on the 28th."
In its infamous office, *Visión* meets
with renegades and ghouls,
Bolivians who lick every dollar
and insult their humble birth,
crucifying Bolivia's hunger
and auctioning off all our lands.
And they meet with other 'Latinos'
likewise surrendered and sinister
who every day spin infernal
lies against Cuba—
it is they alone who prepare this dish.
In this restaurant there is no menu,
they simply add a sauce to the calumny
and serve it up: they're kitchen boys and busboys.
And this dish consisting of bomb raids,
massacres of women and children,
another Batista with a new name,
is prepared far off:

"Nothing is happening here," is what they say.
"The rest we'll take care of with money."
But this time they will pay with their own blood.
This time they will not win over any but the dead.

XXII

SUCH IS MY LIFE

My duties walk with my song.
I am I am not: this is who I am.
I am not if I don't try to ease the sorrows
of those who suffer: they are my sorrows.
I am not unless I am for all,
for all the silenced and exploited.
I come from the people and I sing for the people.
My poetry is a song and a scourge.
They say to me: you belong to the darkness.
Perhaps, perhaps so, but I'm walking toward the light.
I am a man of bread and fish
you won't find me among books,
but with women and men:
it is they who have taught me the infinite.

XXIII

FOR VENEZUELA

I loved Venezuela but she is gone.
I looked for her among the names that lived:
I called and called, no one answered.
The buried nation did not answer.
And yet my map graced her with
a geography of emeralds, mountains
with birds the color of snow,
a blue fire protected her islands,
oil warmed her hips
and embroidered her linings with gold,
the Orinoco was an eternal letter
full of crocodiles and news,
in fact, in fact, Venezuela sounded
like an exquisite hardware store
with diamonds, waterfalls and tapirs
breathing with Simón Bolívar
(meanwhile a gentleman arrived in Chile
to drive us crazy with his orthography).
Thus I walked through the world
knocking on friendly and hostile doors
and every nation had arranged itself
for my visit just as I'd seen them
on the map when I was a boy:
green Asia, carnivorous England,
Spain was inaugurating her graves,

fragrant France was wearing next to nothing,
Switzerland was like a watch among madmen,
Germany was practicing artillery,
Russia changed its given name and surname,
God was living in Rome and suffering—
meanwhile I was searching day after day
for Venezuela without finding her. . .
until Picón Salas from Caracas
came and explained to me what had happened.

XXIV

THE TIGER

Gómez was the name of emptiness
and Gómez was the name of that death.
In just half an hour he auctioned off
the oil to North American gangsters
and has lacked for nothing ever since.
And Venezuela, silently,
sank into the darkness of prisons,
grew sick from hard labor and fever.
Those who were to be my brothers
were forced down harsh roads
excavating rocks and dragging shackles:
ardent Venezuela was bleeding.
Gabaldón related to me how from his cell
he heard an insurgent die:
the worms ate him alive
he could hear his comrade groaning
but wasn't sure what was happening
until those brief, cruel cries
ended. This was Venezuela's
silence: no one answered.
The worms and death thrived.

XXV

PÉREZ JIMÉNEZ

Freedom with Medina Angarita
decorum with Rómulo Gallegos
crossed Venezuela escaping
like birds from other lands in flight
and the beasts of terror returned
to raise fear and devour.
The pregnant night gave birth to
Pérez Jiménez, the Bat:
bulging of soul with a pestilent
belly, a thief and circumflex,
a fat lizard of the swamp,
a gnawing monkey, an obese parrot,
an unsavory pimp,
a cross between a toad and a crab,
Trujillo's and Somoza's bastard
bred in the State Department
for the internal use of monopolies
for whom he was a yellow doormat,
an ambiguous by-product of oil
and a voracious shark of excrement.
This hypocritical swamp toad
devoted himself solely to his own fortune—
outside, all medals and epaulets
nothing but property and dollars inside—
this fierce soldier who never saw war

alone promoted himself to succulent ranks.
But enough of this picturesque
farce as though this were a contest.
But Pérez Jiménez did bury
Venezuela and brutally torture her.
Her grocery stores were filled with pain,
broken limbs, separated bones,
and once again the prisons were
brimming with the most honest men.
Thus the past returned to Venezuela
to lash its bloody whip
until through the streets of Caracas
bullhorns resounded on the wind,
until the walls of the tyrant were smashed
and the people unleashed their majesty.
The rest is the same old and new
miserable history of our time:
the tyrant ran in the middle of the night
like a sleepwalking rabbit to Miami:
there he owns a mansion and there
the Free World welcomed him with open arms.

XXVI

A FOREIGN DEMOCRAT

Betancourt sat on Venezuela's
hopes like a heavy load.
This gentleman—square on the outside
and opaque like cheese inside—
worked hard to be president
(but to be a man he never had time).
Finally in New York they awarded him degrees
in law and government.
Recommended by Muñoz Marín,
the gringos studied him for a minute,
deposited him in Caracas and
sealed him with their perspective.
He learned English to carry out their orders
and in everything he was prompt and circumspect.
While his eyes and ears always faced North America,
toward Venezuela he was deaf and blind.
He'd order his pants from a North American
tailor and even ask him what he thought,
until able to speak with the Voice of his Master
he forgot Venezuela and her people altogether.
Cuba, though, posed a problem,
because of Fidel he was losing sleep:
all those reforms, granting land
to anyone who'd work it—how embarrassing!
and providing housing for every Cuban—

[51]

Cuba's going straight to hell!
and selling sugar to whomever buys it—
how intolerably audacious!
Poor Betancourt soon became
the sad Cain of our time.
Then, in Caracas, an insurrection
of gentle youth flowered:
those insubordinate students
entrenched themselves in their discontent.
Betancourt, the warrior, immediately sent in
his police and regiments,
his tanks, his planes, his iron
and mowed down defenseless kids.
In front of the schools in mourning,
amid blackboards and notebooks,
this "North American" democrat
left dozens of kids dead.
Once again Venezuela bathed in blood.
Herod Betancourt kept silent.

XXVII

BIRDS OF THE CARIBBEAN

During this brief gust of wind
sweeping away human concerns,
I invite you to celebrate the birds—
the martin, swift windsail,
the dazzling light of the hummingbird,
housecleaner that divides the sky in two
for the most shadowy crane
until the hands of dawn
weave together the colors of the *aguaitacaminos*.
Oh birds, precious stones of the Caribbean,
quetzal, Paradise's nuptial ray of light,
the air's jewelry adorning the foliage,
yellow birds the color of lightning bolts
mixed with drops of turquoise
and the fire of naked cataclisms:
come to my small human song.
Water troupial, simple partridge,
thrushes of miraculous form,
earthy *chocorocay*,
delicate golden dancers on the air,
ultraviolet, thread-tailed tintora,
rock roosters, water birds,
compañeros, mysterious friends,
how did the feather surpass the flower?
Golden Mask, unconquered woodpecker,

what must I do to sing in the midst of
your Venezuela, beside your nests,
your splendor of celestial semaphores,
your martins, fishermen of the dew,
if from the extreme South my voice
is opaque, the voice of a somber heart,
and I am but a stone on the Caribbean sand
that arrived from the cold?
How to sing the song,
the foliage, the light, the power
of what I saw in disbelief
or heard not believing what I heard?
when a flock of red herons flying over me
like a flowing red river in flight
against the Venezuelan radiance
of a burning sapphire-blue sun,
surged like an eclipse of beauty:
such a ceremony!
If you didn't see the crimson of the *corocoro*
flying in a suspended swarm, slicing
through the light like a scythe
and the whole sky shaking in flight
and the passing scarlet feathers
igniting a bolt of lightning,
if you did not see the Caribbean air
flowing with blood without being wounded,
you do not know the beauty of this world,
you know nothing of the world in which you live.
This is why I speak and why I sing
why I see and live through every man:

it is my duty to sing of what you do not know,
and what you do know I will sing with you:
your eyes accompany my words
and my words multiply in the wheat
and fly with the wings of the Caribbean
or fight your enemies.
I have so many duties, compañeros,
I must now turn to another subject and say so long.

XXVIII

WRETCHED EVENTS

If New York glitters like gold
and buildings there have five hundred bars,
let me state here and now they were made
off the sweat in the canefields.
The banana plantation is a green inferno
so people may drink and dance in New York.
Chileans spit up blood
at an altitude of five thousand meters
so copper may be exported to New York,
Bolivians collapse from hunger
gouging out tin mines,
breaking through Andean walls,
and the Orinoco scatters its diamonds
from the depths of its muddy bottom.
Through stolen Panamanian land,
through stolen waters, ships pass
on their way to New York with our oil,
with our seized minerals
that our decorated leaders
reverently handed over to them.
Sugar raises the walls,
Chile's nitrate the cities,
Brazil's coffee buys beds,
Paraguay grants them universities,
from Colombia they receive emeralds,

and from Puerto Rico,
that Free Associated State,
soldiers leave for their wars
(for battles fought like none other:
North Americans supply the weapons
Puerto Ricans supply the blood).

XXIX

DON'T TELL ME

Some people tell me not to deal with this
matter of humans, people with names,
surnames and sorrows in the pages of my books,
not to give them space in my poems.
They say poetry died here.
Some say I mustn't do it.
Truth is I have no desire to please them.
I greet them, even tip my hat to them,
and I leave them strolling on Parnassus
like happy rats on cheese.
I belong to a different category,
I am a mere man of flesh and blood.
Therefore if they beat on my brother
I defend him with whatever I have in hand
and each one of my lines carries
the threat of gunpowder or iron
that will come down on the inhuman,
on the cruel, on the haughty and arrogant.
But the retribution for my furious peace
threatens neither the poor nor the good:
With my lamp I go searching for the fallen,
I soothe their wounds and I close them.
This is the work of the poet,
of the aviator, of the stonecutter.
We must make something of this earth

because unto this planet we were born,
and the things of men must be set in order
because we are neither birds nor dogs.
So, if when I attack what I loathe
or when I sing to all those I love,
poetry wants to abandon
the hope contained in my manifesto,
I will follow the letter of my law
accumulating stars and armaments,
and in my unshakeable duty to America
one rose more or less does not matter:
I have made a pact of love with beauty.
I have made a pact of blood with my people.

XXX

OAS MEETING

No one really cares whether or not
you are schooled in diplomacy,
but this science does have its subtle twists,
its frozen or infernal thickets,
and today I must open the eyes of the just
to teach what everyone already knows
and demonstrate just how far our gathered
nations can untangle themselves,
and not be just furniture
for Uncle Sam to sit on.
Our gathered ambassadors
form a soft silk cushion
for that sacrosanct bottom:
Argentina offers its wool,
Ecuador its best macaw,
Peru its ancestral llamas,
Santo Domingo sends its nephews,
brothers-in-law and other animals.
Chile is original like no other
and designates as representative
a bottle of wine without wine
or an inkless inkwell filled with vinegar.
Thus these gentlemen prepare
for their long, unspeakable meetings.
They balance themselves one on top of the other

employing very interesting acrobatics
in order to fight to be the first seat.
"They should at least step all over me"
demands the delegate from Colombia
writing a sonnet, crossing himself,
while the delegates from Paraguay
and El Salvador, without scraping each other,
want to be exclusive seats,
and express their reasons in such a way
that everyone is moved, but
just at this critical juncture
in walks their North American Chief:
he of course sits on everyone without paying
the slightest attention to who he sat on first.
Dead silence fills the room.
The Chief under pressure dictates accord
and goes back to his important affairs.
Our ambassadors regain their composure,
straighten their elegant suits,
and this meeting is over.
Gentlemen, the OAS has its faults
but they are deliciously unanimous.

XXXI

1960 EXPLOSION OF THE *COUBRE*

My subject is this ship that arrived
loaded with munitions and happiness:
its cargo exploded in Havana,
the sea on fire was its agony.
Two different Eisenhowers were
at work in this together:
one who navigated underwater
the other who smiled in Argentina,
one who set the explosive
the other who decorated whomever was in power,
one who pushed the torpedo button
the other who lied to all America,
one who swam like a green octopus
the other who was more charming than an aunt.
These two accomplices
had learned that our geography
is managed by rootless governors
who relinguished their sovereignty—
for them North America is
not always an empty cash box.
So they give it their all:
false hopes, the police,
President Eisenhower strolling
through palaces and down streets
without meeting one real person—

only voracious tigers in business suits
who want to sell him our flags.
But in the USA it is widely known
that one talks differently with Fidel
and when in Cuba they see peasants
for the first time in the light of the word,
with their newly received dignity,
their books and their land.
A pasty-faced Eisenhower removes
his good-guy mask, transforms himself
into a frogman and swims
like a shark toward its prey.
Then the assassinated *Coubre*
writhes in cinders with her wounded:
they murder Frenchmen and Cubans
for these North American leaders,
but this time the bandit submarines
had no cause afterwards for revelry
because they will never murder Cuba.
She will live on, this star, we swear it:
we will fight for her revolution
until the last hand, defending
her honor, casts the last stone.

XXXII

THE AMERICAS

Viva! Colombia beautiful and mournful,
and Ecaudor crowned by fire,
Viva! small wounded Paraguay
resurrected by naked heroes,
O Venezuela, you sing on the map
with the immense blue sky in motion,
and I celebrate Bolivia's rugged mountains,
her Indian eyes and festive light.
I know the people fell here and there
defending their honor, our honor,
and I love even the roots of my land
from the Rio Grande to the Chilean Pole
not only because our bones are scattered
wide throughout this long struggle,
but because I love every humble door
and every hand of our profound peoples.
There is no beauty like this beauty
of America stretched across its infernos,
its rocky and powerful mountains,
its pristine and eternal rivers,
and I love you in the deepest spaces
of the cities smelling of dung,
in the trains at flickering dawn,
in the markets and in the slaughterhouses,
in the electric flowers of your images of saints,

in the cruel construction of your crabs,
in your decapitated miner
and your poor turbulent drunk.
The planet gave all of you snow,
waterways and new volcanoes.
Later on, man went adding walls
and inside the walls, suffering.
In love I press up against your flanks:
receive me as though I were the wind.
I bring you a song that strikes
an unquenchable love
and the fertilization of bells:
the justice that our peoples yearn for.
It's not much to ask, we have so much,
and yet we have so little
it is impossible for this to continue.
This is my song, what I ask is this:
Because I can only ask for all,
I ask all for our peoples,
and let the conceited wretch
mad with ambition be offended.
I will press on accompanied by
my heart and my suffering.

XXXIII

HISTORY OF A CANAL

Panama, geography granted you
a gift no other land was given:
two oceans advanced to meet you,
and the cordillera narrowed and descended.
Instead of one ocean it gave you
two sovereigns of salt spray:
the Atlantic kisses you with lips
accustomed to kissing grapes,
while the Pacific thrashes
its cyclonic stature in your honor.
So, tiny Panama, little sister,
I am having my first doubts now:
I'll whisper them in your ear for I believe
one must speak of bitterness very quietly.
What happened, little sister? They cut
up your figure as though it were cheese
and then ate and left you
like a gnawed olive pit.
Much later I learned the canal
was made like a river on the moon:
through that river the world would arrive
spilling fortunes on the sand.
But others from another part of the world
fastened their yoke on you,
mortgaged your waist,

and spilled nothing but whiskey.
So everything is going as was planned
by these devils and their imposters:
with their money they made the Canal,
with your blood they dug the earth
and now they send dollars to New York
leaving you the graves.

XXXIV

FUTURE OF A CANAL

Water slices through you like a knife
dividing love in two
with the iciness of dollars invested
to the hilt in your honeycombs—
I'm telling you the pain I feel.
If others do not see these crimes
you will think I'm simply lost or that
I drank too many beers in your bars,
but these constructions, these lakes,
these blue waters of two oceans
must not be the blade that divides
the miserable from the happy.
The doorway of this salt spray must be
the great union of two nuptial worlds—
a narrow pathway constructed
for men, not crocodiles,
for love, not money,
not for hatred but for bread,
and I have to say that this canal
and every canal built on your
territory belongs to you—
these are your sacred fountains.
The ocean currents that surround you
are yours, they are your veins,
and the vampires who devour them

must pack their bags and leave.
Your seagoing flag alone
must fly in the afternoon wind:
the Panamian wind that asks
like a child who's lost her mother
where is the flag of my homeland?
She is waiting. And Panama knows it.
And we Americans know it
from Patagonia to the Río Grande.
One flag alone over the Canal
must wave its fragrant petal—
not the skull-and-crossbones,
but one more rose of our blood.
The pure flag of Panama
will preside over the passage of ships.

XXXV

THE "FREE" PRESS

During this brief chilly spell
I want to relate to you,
without vengeance, with joy even,
how from my bed in Buenos Aires
the police took me off to prison.
It was evening, we had just arrived from Chile
and without saying a word to us
they rifled through my friend's papers,
plundered the house in which I slept.
My wife flashed her scorn
but orders are orders
and so in a roving car we toured
the black night of tyranny.
Back then it wasn't Perón, but another,
a new kingpin for Argentina,
and his orders opened doors,
bolt after bolt after bolt opened
to swallow me up, we passed courtyards,
forty jails and the infirmary,
but still they led me up to a cell,
the most impenetrable, secret cell:
only there did they believe they were safe
from the vapors of my poetry.
During that shattered night I learned
three thousand had been imprisoned that day:

prisons, penitentiaries, and when these were full
they set ships adrift at sea
filled with men and women,
the proud souls of Argentina.
Well, my tale stops here,
the rest is collective history:
I wanted to read about it in the newspapers
in *La Prensa* (which is so informative)
but Mr. Gaínza Paz was unaware
Argentina's prisons were brimming over.
He is the champion of our "free" press
but if they close the communist dailies
this great man suddenly knows nothing,
writes nothing, his shoes are killing him,
his eyes can't focus, and if the workers
are rounded up and sent to prison
everyone knows about it,
everyone, that is, but Gaínza.
Everyone relies on the newspapers,
but the "great" dailies won't publish
a thing about these ridiculous tales:
La Prensa was extremely busy
with the lastest Hollywood divorce
of two asinine movie stars,
and at the same time the unions are under attack
La Prensa and *La Nación* are metaphysical.
Ay! what silence from the fat press
when the people receive a beating,
but if one of Batista's jackals
is gunned down in Cuba,

the presses of our poor America
raise their hands to their temples,
prepare and print their juicy stories—
Oh yes, they know what to publish!
The Sip, Sop, Sep meets
to save the vestal virgins in danger,
and running to their Purse in New York
they hurriedly solicit
the ever jingling incentives
for the "freedom" they patronize.
These unseemly web-footed men
infest all of Latin America,
they kiss Chamudes in Santiago,
Judas Ravines waits for them in Lima,
and later they are enriched and inspired
by that so-called freedom exhaled from
Washington where a rock & roll tune plays
and they dance with Dubois and Gaínza.

XXXVI

DANCING WITH BLACKS

Blacks of the continent, you brought
what had been missing to the New World:
without blacks the drums don't breathe
without blacks the guitars don't play.
Our green Americas were motionless
until they moved like palm trees
when the dance of blood and grace
was born of a black couple.
After suffering so much misery—
cutting cane till you die
looking after pigs in forests
lugging heavy boulders
washing pyramids of clothes
climbing stairs loaded down
stopping on the road alone
having neither plate nor spoon
earning more beatings than your wage
suffering the sale of your sister
grinding flower for an entire century
eating but one day a week
running and running like a horse
delivering crates of sandals,
pushing a broom and working a saw,
digging out mountains, excavating roads,
then lying down exhausted, with death,

and up and living again each morning—
you are singing as no one can sing
singing with your body and soul.
Oh to say this! my heart
my life and my words are torn apart
and I cannot go on because I prefer
to go with the African palms
keepers of our terrestrial music that now
from my window fills me with excitement:
I am going out to dance through the streets
with my black brothers of Havana.

XXXVII

A PROFESSOR DISAPPEARS

In New York a stray odor of cheese
wafts over the fake gardenias:
from 42nd street out to Long Island
it covers every wintry thing
and the classroom shivered
going suddenly from heat to dead cold.
Our friend emerged from there
wrapped in air as bitter as his exile,
but urban North America had now
wrapped him in its new overcoat:
he thought it would give free reign to
the ancestral role of his memories.
The professor's name was Galíndez
and that night he went to hell.
They beat him over the head
and took him unconscious
through the night, the streets,
through the abandoned airport
to Santo Domingo, where a pale ruffian
with the face of an old man reigns,
a demonic monkey propped up
by the State Department.
In shackles, they brought the wretched
professor with his memories to the throne—
it is not known if he was burned alive

or slowly, limb by limb, torn apart
or cut into little pieces
or roasted in the blood of other dead men,
but before the assembled Court
the professor was sent to his torment:
they paid the pilot (a North American
of course) right there on the spot,
the puppet despot carried on in Santo Domingo,
and in New York winter continues.

XXXVIII

THE HEROES

On this ship that is a bloody swamp
many were wounded and killed:
the wretched abyss swallowed them
with its tortures and its prisoners.
For this fortress of the cruel
there are bullets and money in Washington
and in Hollywood Trujillo's son
is a leading man, a total gentleman.
But the students who fire
against evil, alone or scattered,
won't find asylum in any embassy
nor will they find ships to board
nor planes to transport them out of the country—
except to where torment awaits them—
they will be denied visas to New York
with the most convincing arguments,
until a young clandestine hero
is later betrayed and discovered:
no eyes will be left in his eyesockets,
one by one they will break his bones.
Afterwards, they will strut about at the UN
in this Free World of ours
as the North American Defense Minister
gives Trujillo new weapons. This story
is horrible, I know, and if you've suffered

you will forgive me, but I do not regret it.
This is how the wicked perpetuate themselves:
this is reality, I am not lying.

XXXIX

TO A NORTH AMERICAN FRIEND

Man of the north, North American,
industrial harvester of apples,
as plain as a pine tree in a pine grove,
geographic evergreen of Alaska,
Yankee of the towns and factories
with a wife, responsibilities and children,
fertile engineers who work
in the immutable jungle of numbers
or in the time clocks of factories,
broad workers, lanky workers and
workers bent over wheels and flames,
heartrending poets who have lost
Whitman's faith in the human race,
I want what I love and what I hate
to remain clear in my words:
my only reproach of you
is for this silence that says nothing:
we have no idea what North Americans
are thinking in their homes.
We love the sweet comfort of the family,
but we also love the sudden flare-up,
when something happens in this world
we want to share in what's been learned,
yet we find that two or three persons
shut the doors of North Americans in our face

and only the Voice of America is heard,
which is like listening to a plucked hen.
But as to the rest, I celebrate here:
your feats of today and tomorrow,
and I think the satellite you sent into
orbit one dawn, even though delayed,
is worthy of everyone's pride:
Why always be the first in everything?
In the championship race of life
boasting has forever remained behind:
thus we can go together to the sun
and drink wine from the same cup.
We are Americans like you,
we don't desire to exclude you from anything,
but we do want to conserve what is ours.
There is plenty of space for all our souls,
we can live without trampling on each other
with an underdeveloped sympathy,
until we can say frankly to one another
how far we have come, face to face.
The world is changing and I don't think
you have to win with bombs and swords.
On this basis let us understand each other
without you having to suffer a thing.
We're not going to exploit your oil,
we won't interfere with customs,
we're not going to sell electricity
to North American towns and cities:
we are peaceful people who can
be content with the little we earn,

we don't want to make anyone
covet the circumstances of others.
We respect Lincoln's place in history
and Paul Robeson's clear conscience.
We learned to love you with Charlie Chaplin
(though his strength was evily rewarded).
And so many things, the geography
that unites us on desired land,
everything compels me to say once again
that we are sailing on the same ship
and it could sink from too much pride:
let us load it with bread and apples,
let us load it with whites and blacks,
with understanding and hope.

XL

TOMORROW THROUGHOUT THE CARIBBEAN

Pure youth of this bloody sea,
young communists of the day:
there will be more of you to clean
our territory of tyrannies
and one day we shall meet,
and in freedom my poetry
will sing again among you.
Comrades, I await this happily.

XLI

ONE MINUTE TO SING FOR THE
SIERRA MAESTRA

If silence is requested to say goodbye
to our own who've returned to dust,
I will request one resounding minute,
for once the whole voice of America,
I ask for only one minute of deep song
to honor the Sierra Maestra. For now
let us put aside the affairs of man:
let us honor this land among so many
that keeps in its mysterious mountains
the spark that would burn on the prairies.
I celebrate the steep canopy of leaves,
the enduring habitat of stones,
the night of indecisive murmurings
with the palpitations of the stars,
the naked silence of the mountains,
the enigma of a people without flags:
until everything started to throb,
bursting suddenly into a fiery blaze.
And invincible bearded men came down
to establish peace over the land—
now everything is bright, but back then
everything was dark in the Sierra Maestra,
which is why I ask for this unanimous minute
to sing with all of you this *Epic Song,*

and I will begin with these words
that they may resound over and over throughout America:
"Open your eyes, offended peoples,
there is a Sierra Maestra in every land."

MEDITATION ON THE SIERRA MAESTRA

XLII

WRITTEN IN THE YEAR 2000

I want to talk with the last stars
now, high on this human mountain,
I am alone with the night, my companion,
and a heart worn down over the years:
This solitude arrived from far away,
I have a right to the sovereign dream,
to rest with my eyes open
among tired, weary eyes,
and while man sleeps with his tribe,
when all eyes are closed—
the peoples plunged into the night,
the sky a starry rose garden—
I let time pass over my face
like the dark air or a teardrenched heart
and I see what's coming and what's being born,
the defeated sorrows,
the humble hopes of my people:
children wearing shoes in school,
bread and justice for all
the way the sun drenches in summer.
I see simplicity fully evolved,
the purity of man with his plow,
and as I come and go among the furrows
I encounter not one sprawling hacienda.
Light is so simple and yet to be discovered:

love seemed so far off,
reason was always nearby:
we were the lost ones
already believing in a wretched world
full of emperors and soldiers,
when suddenly it was seen that
the cruel and wicked were gone forever,
and everyone was at peace
in their homes, on the streets, working.
And now we all know it is wrong
for the land to be in the hands of a few,
that there's no need to go running frantically
between governors and courts.
How simple peace is and yet how difficult
assaulted by stones and sticks
every day and every night,
as though we were no longer Christians.
The night is deep and pure as stone
and it touches my rib with its cold
as though telling me to quickly fall asleep,
that my work is now done.
But I must talk with the stars
in a dark and clear language,
and with the night itself, speaking
plainly brother to brother.
The night envelops me with a strong fragrance
and touches me with its hands:
I realize I am that nocturne
I left behind in the distant past
when youthful spring

throbbed under my provincial shirt:
All the love of that lost time,
the sorrow of a wrested aroma,
the color of a street covered in ashes,
the inextinguishable sky of a few hands!
And later, those devouring climates
where my heart was devoured,
ships fleeing with no destination,
obscure or ravaged countries,
that fever I had in Burma
and the love that was crucified.
I am only a man and I bear my afflictions
as any mortal saddened from loving
loving loving without being loved
and from not loving having been loved.
The ashes of one night appear
near the sea, upon a sacred river,
and the dark corpse of a woman
is burning in an abandoned hearth:
from its dense thickets the Irrawaddy River
moves its water and light like a shark.
The fishermen of Ceylon who raised
with me the whole ocean and its fish,
their nets alive and dripping
with miraculous velvety-red fish
while the elephants waited
for me to offer them fruit from my palms.
Ay! how much time has accumulated
on my brow like an opaque clock
that carries in its delicate movement

one interminably long thread
that begins with a child crying
and ends with a wanderer and his sack!
Then came war and its pain:
the dead Spaniards touch my eyes
and search for me in the night,
and I search for them but they don't see me,
and yet I can see their extinguished light:
Don Antonio dying without hope,
Miguel Hernández dead in his prisons,
and poor Federico assassinated
by sinister medieval men,
by the unfaithful followers of Paneros:
assassins of nightingales!
Ay! so much, so much darkness, so much blood!
They are calling me tonight by my name:
they touch me now with frozen wings
and show me their enormous martyrdom:
no one has avenged them and they ask this of me:
Yes, only my tenderness knows them.
Ay! how much night there is in one night
without this celestial cup spilling over,
the silence of distances sounds
like an impenetrable seashell
and the stars fall into my hands
still full of music and shadow.
In this space the tumultuous weight
of my life neither crushes nor sobs
and I bid farewell to the pain that visits me
the way I would say goodbye to a dove:

if there are scores to settle, they must be settled
with what is to come and is being born,
with the whole world's happiness
and not with what time wears down.
And here under the Sierra Maestra sky
I rise alone to salute the dawn
because I came late to my duties.
I spent life on so many things
that I leave my work to others' hands
and another's mouth will sing my song—
thus workday is joined to workday
and thus the rose will continue flowering.
Man does not stop on his journey,
another takes up mysterious arms,
the human spring flows endlessly,
the butterfly was born of winter
more delicate than a flower,
which is why her beauty knows no repose
and her dazzling colorful wings open and close
in precise mathematical symmetry.
And one man built a door
with but one drop from the sea
until from one life to another life
we will raise a happy city
with the arms of those who no longer live
and the hands of those yet to be born.
This is the unity we will achieve:
light organized by darkness,
by the continuity of human desire
and time advancing the hours

until we all are content.
And so, history begins once again.
And so, in the heights of these mountains,
far from Chile and her cordilleras,
I receive my past in a cup
and raise it over the entire earth,
and though my country circulates in my blood
her fountain never ceasing,
at this hour my nocturnal reasoning
situates in Cuba the common flag
of our dark hemisphere that
awaited true victory at last.
I leave it on this summit, safeguarded,
upright, waving high over the prairies,
to remind the exploited peoples
of the dignity born of struggle:
Cuba is a tall and clear mast observed
across every space and every darkness,
she is like a tree born at the center
of the Caribbean Sea and its ancient sorrows:
her foliage is seen in every corner
and her seeds fall to the ground,
raising throughout somber America
the edifice of spring.

XLIII

FINAL JUDGMENT

If in the duration of pain and sorrows
there is a suffocation, a breathless gasp
of fear that wells up in the soul
until our cup of dread is full,
there is in what man does, in his victories,
a branch of pure disillusionment
that grows without birds or petals:
watered not by rain, but by tears.

This book, the first among poetry books
to extol the Cuban intention,
this *Epic Song* whose only
reason to be is hope
was attacked by wretched writers
who in Cuba never liberated a thing
except their own bank accounts
that were defended by the revolution.

I knew one once, a cynical black man,
who, passing himself off as a comrade,
would go from cabaret to cabaret
in Paris winning all the latest battles
so that he could arrive smug as ever
in Havana to collect his laurels.

And I knew another, an eternally neutral
man who, fleeing the Nazis like a rat,
then behaved like a hero and was silent
when his voice was most needed.

And another so much retamar that stripped
of his fernández he's now worth nothing
except the price Cubans pay for
his selling elegies and buying fame.

Ay Cuba! Your people are defending your
enduring radiant star with their arms!

While Miami welcomes its *gusanos*
your own writers undermine you
and the one who realizes things
and participates in the common battle
distinguishes those who fight face-to-face
against North American rage
from those who spend their peoples' ink
dousing the spark of solidarity.

But we know that over time
the face of that masked writer
Envy falls from combat
and we see the withered flesh,
we see the lying conceits,
and we see the mercenary hands.

At this hour we see everything.

From this moment on I sound the bells
announcing the Final Judgment of our conscience.

I will arrive with my conscience clear.

I will arrive with my song,
with what my party has taught me:
I will arrive, Cuba, with the same slow eyes,
the same voice and the same face
to defend before death's insult
your revolutionary epic.